General Knowledge

1) Who scored the first goal of the century for Brighton, in a 4-2 win over Exeter in January 2000?

2) Who was the team's main kit sponsor in 2012/13 before American Express took over the following year?

3) Which player was top scorer for Brighton in the 2015/16 Championship season?

4) Brighton won back-to-back league titles in which two seasons this century?

5) Lewis Dunk made his debut in a League One match versus which team in 2010?

6) Who became the first player from Cameroon to play for the club when he signed in 2015?

7) Which player became the club's youngest ever player when he debuted in a match versus Yeovil in May 2010?

8) Who became the oldest player to represent Brighton when he played aged 44 years and 1 month old against Grimsby in May 2003?

9) Which squad number has Solly March worn at the club since the 2015/16 season?

10) Bruno replaced which player as Brighton captain ahead of the 2016/17 season?

11) Against which side did Bruno make his final appearance for the Seagulls?

12) Who scored the only goal in the 2004 Division Two Play-Off Final win over Bristol City?

13) Who scored an unfortunate own goal in the 3-3 draw with Wolves in January 2021?

14) Brighton claimed a vital 2-1 win over Sheffield Wednesday in the Championship in January 2017 thanks in part to a penalty save from which goalkeeper?

15) Which team did Brighton beat on penalties in the FA Cup Third Round in 2012?

16) Which team did Brighton play and what was the final score in the last game played at the Withdean in 2011?

17) Who scored twice late on to secure a 2-1 win over Doncaster Rovers in the first competitive match at the Amex Stadium?

18) Which team tore Brighton apart in beating them 7-1 in August 2009?

19) Who scored a hat-trick in the 5-0 win over Norwich in October 2016?

20) Which Brighton player was dismissed for tripping up the referee during the loss to Bolton in March 2013?

21) Which Aston Villa player scored against Brighton in the last minute of the 2016/17 Championship season to deny the Seagulls the league title?

22) Which team finished second behind Brighton in the 2010/11 League One table?

Transfers 2000-2010

1) Nathan Jones signed from which club in July 2000?

2) Which striker was bought from Bristol Rovers in August 2000?

3) Who did Mark Walton sign for on a free transfer in July 2000?

4) Which German signed from Hibernian in the summer of 2001?

5) Which club did Andy Crosby join from Brighton in December 2001?

6) Brighton signed which striker on a free from West Ham in August 2002?

7) From which Premier League side was Leon Knight purchased in 2003?

8) Dave Beasant left to join who in the summer of 2003?

9) Which striker signed for Brighton for one month from Weymouth in 2004, before leaving for Brentford?

10) Brighton signed which player from Monaco in August 2005?

11) Who was sold to Celtic at the end of the 2004/05 season?

12) From which team was Nicky Forster bought in June 2007?

13) Which forward left for Sheffield United in the summer of 2006?

14) Brighton brought in Glenn Murray from which club in January 2008?

15) Who was sold to Colchester United in the 2008 January transfer window?

16) Chris Birchall signed from where in January 2009?

17) Striker Craig Davies was brought in from which team in 2009?

18) Andrew Crofts left after one season in 2010 to sign for which side?

19) From which club did Brighton sign Ashley Barnes in 2010?

20) Which two players arrived from Stockport in July 2009?

Cup Games

1) Brighton lost to eventually FA Cup winners Leicester in 2021 by what score in the Fifth Round?

2) By what score did Brighton beat Portsmouth in the League Cup in September 2020?

3) Which team knocked Brighton out of the EFL Trophy at the Quarter Final stage in 2008?

4) Which Manchester City scored the only goal as Brighton lost in the 2019 FA Cup Semi Final?

5) Brighton had reached that stage by dramatically beating Millwall on penalties in the Quarter Final having drawn 2-2 in normal time thanks to late goals from which two players?

6) Which lower-league club knocked Brighton out of the FA Cup at the First Round stage in November 2003?

7) Who scored two own goals during the 6-1 FA Cup defeat to Liverpool in February 2012?

8) Which League Two team beat Brighton in the League Cup in August 2013?

9) Which team did Brighton hammer 8-0 in the FA Cup in 2006?

10) Which Premier League side did Brighton knock out of the FA Cup in both 2012 and 2013?

Memorable Games

1) Who scored the winner as Brighton won 2-1 at Crystal Palace in March 2019?

2) Which team did Brighton beat 5-0 at home in League One in March 2009?

3) Which Manchester City player was sent off before The Seagulls fought back from 2-0 down to win 3-2 in May 2021?

4) Who scored the equaliser against Ipswich on the final day of the 2004/05 Championship season to ensure the club avoided the drop?

5) Who scored a hat-trick as Brighton beat Leyton Orient 5-0 on New Year's Day in 2011?

6) Brighton beat Fulham 5-0 in April 2016 thanks to a hat-trick from Tomer Hemed, and goals from Anthony Knockaert and which other player?

7) By what score-line did Brighton beat Blackpool at home in the Championship in April 2013?

8) Which defender scored the only goal as Crystal Palace were beaten 1-0 at Selhurst Park in October 2005?

9) Bobby Zamora scored three times in an entertaining 6-2 win over which team in September 2000?

10) Who scored twice during the 3-0 win over Spurs in October 2019?

Red Cards

1) Which two Brighton players were sent off during the 2-1 defeat at Wolves in May 2021?

2) Who was given his marching orders following a tangle with Adebayo Akinfenwa in a 1-1 draw with Northampton in 2009?

3) Lewis Dunk was sent off late on in the 1-1 draw with Crystal Palace in October 2020 for a lunge on which player?

4) Gary Hart was dismissed for elbowing an opposition player in a 3-2 defeat to which team in February 2003?

5) Brighton lost 3-0 to which side in February 2006 after Adam Hinshelwood was shown two yellow cards?

6) Who was shown a straight red for a reckless challenge in the 2-0 home loss to Southampton in August 2019?

7) Who scored but was then dismissed in the 1-1 Championship draw with Middlesbrough in 2016?

8) Andrew Crofts was sent off against which Championship club in August 2014?

9) Brighton managed to beat Crystal Palace 3-1 in December 2018 despite which defender being shown a red card in the first half?

10) Ben White was sent off against which team in April 2021?

Managers

1) Who was the Brighton manager at the start of the 21st century?

2) What was the result in Steve Coppell's last game in charge before he left for Reading?

3) Who took over as permanent manager from Coppell in 2003?

4) Who was in charge as Brighton avoided relegation from League One in 2009?

5) Which team did Brighton beat 3-1 away from home in Gus Poyet's first game as manager?

6) Gus Poyet was replaced as manager by who in 2013?

7) Who was placed in caretaker charge after Sami Hyypia left the club?

8) Chris Hughton appointed who as his assistant manager in February 2015?

9) Hughton guided the club to their first ever Premier League win with victory over which team in September 2017?

10) Graham Potter started off his reign with a victory away at Watford by what score-line?

First Goals

Can you name the club that these players scored their first goal for the club against?

1) Bobby Zamora

2) Leon Knight

3) Colin Kazim-Richards

4) Glenn Murray

5) Lewis Dunk

6) Leonard Ulloa

7) Ashley Barnes

8) Anthony Knockaert

9) Neal Maupay

10) Alireza Jahanbakhsh

Transfers 2011-2021

1) From which team did Brighton buy Will Buckley in June 2011?

2) Which Dutch forward signed from Excelsior in July 2011?

3) From which club did Will Hoskins arrive on a free in 2011?

4) Club legend Bruno was signed back in 2012 from which Spanish side?

5) Who was sold to Cardiff City in August 2012?

6) Matthew Upson signed on a free transfer from which club in 2013?

7) Who was sold to Sunderland in the January transfer window of 2014?

8) Which goalkeeper arrived from Fulham in 2014?

9) Which two players left to join Leicester City in July 2014?

10) Brighton bought which Shrewsbury player in August 2015?

11) From which club was Pascal Gross bought in May 2017?

12) Goalkeeper Matt Ryan arrived from which team in 2017?

13) Who arrived from Viktoria Plzen in the summer of 2017?

14) Which club did Kazenga Lua Lua leave for in January 2018?

15) From which club was Alireza Jahanbakhsh bought in July 2018?

16) Who was sold to Sheffield United in the winter transfer window of 2019?

17) Brighton signed which player from PSG in August 2019?

18) Aaron Mooy left to join which Chinese team in 2020?

19) Jose Izquierdo joined which team on a free after leaving Brighton in 2021?

20) Which player signed from Ajax in July 2021?

Answers

General Knowledge Answers

1) Who scored the first goal of the century for Brighton, in a 4-2 win over Exeter in January 2000?
Darren Freeman

2) Who was the team's main kit sponsor in 2012/13 before American Express took over the following year?
Brighton and Hove Jobs.com

3) Which player was top scorer for Brighton in the 2015/16 Championship season?
Tomer Hemed

4) Brighton won back-to-back league titles in which two seasons this century?
2000/01 (Division Three) and 2001/02 (Division Two)

5) Lewis Dunk made his debut in a League One match versus which team in 2010?
MK Dons

6) Who became the first player from Cameroon to play for the club when he signed in 2015?
Gaetan Bong

7) Which player became the club's youngest ever player when he debuted in a match versus Yeovil in May 2010?
Jake Forster-Caskey

8) Who became the oldest player to represent Brighton when he played aged 44 years and 1 month old against Grimsby in May 2003?
Dave Beasant

9) Which squad number has Solly March worn at the club since the 2015/16 season?
20

10) Bruno replaced which player as Brighton captain ahead of the 2016/17 season?
Gordon Greer

11) Against which side did Bruno make his final appearance for the Seagulls?
Manchester City

12) Who scored the only goal in the 2004 Division Two Play-Off Final win over Bristol City?
Leon Knight

13) Who scored an unfortunate own goal in the 3-3 draw with Wolves in January 2021?
Dan Burn

14) Brighton claimed a vital 2-1 win over Sheffield Wednesday in the Championship in January 2017 thanks in part to a penalty save from which goalkeeper?
David Stockdale

15) Which team did Brighton beat on penalties in the FA Cup Third Round in 2012?
Wrexham

16) Which team did Brighton play and what was the final score in the last game played at the Withdean in 2011?
Brighton 2-3 Huddersfield Town

17) Who scored twice late on to secure a 2-1 win over Doncaster Rovers in the first competitive match at the Amex Stadium?
Will Buckley

18) Which team tore Brighton apart in beating them 7-1 in August 2009?
Huddersfield Town

19) Who scored a hat-trick in the 5-0 win over Norwich in October 2016?
Glenn Murray

20) Which Brighton player was dismissed for tripping up the referee during the loss to Bolton in March 2013?
Ashley Barnes

21) Which Aston Villa player scored against Brighton in the last minute of the 2016/17 Championship season to deny the Seagulls the league title?
Jack Grealish

22) Which team finished second behind Brighton in the 2010/11 League One table?
Southampton

Transfers 2000-2010 Answers

1) Nathan Jones signed from which club in July 2000?
Southend

2) Which striker was bought from Bristol Rovers in August 2000?
Bobby Zamora

3) Who did Mark Walton sign for on a free transfer in July 2000?
Cardiff City

4) Which German signed from Hibernian in the summer of 2001?
Dirk Lehmann

5) Which club did Andy Crosby join from Brighton in December 2001?
Oxford United

6) Brighton signed which striker on a free from West Ham in August 2002?
Paul Kitson

7) From which Premier League side was Leon Knight purchased in 2003?
Chelsea

8) Dave Beasant left to join who in the summer of 2003?
Fulham

9) Which striker signed for Brighton for one month from Weymouth in 2004, before leaving for Brentford?
Steve Claridge

10) Brighton signed which player from Monaco in August 2005?
Sebastien Carole

11) Who was sold to Celtic at the end of the 2004/05 season?
Adam Virgo

12) From which team was Nicky Forster bought in June 2007?
Hull City

13) Which forward left for Sheffield United in the summer of 2006?
Colin Kazim-Richards

14) Brighton brought in Glenn Murray from which club in January 2008?
Rochdale

15) Who was sold to Colchester United in the 2008 January transfer window?
Dean Hammond

16) Chris Birchall signed from where in January 2009?
Coventry City

17) Striker Craig Davies was brought in from which team in 2009?
Oldham Athletic

18) Andrew Crofts left after one season in 2010 to sign for which side?
Norwich City

19) From which club did Brighton sign Ashley Barnes in 2010?

Plymouth

20) Which two players arrived from Stockport in July 2009?

James Tunnicliffe and Gary Dicker

Cup Games Answers

1) Brighton lost to eventually FA Cup winners Leicester in 2021 by what score in the Fifth Round?
Brighton 0-1 Leicester City

2) By what score did Brighton beat Portsmouth in the League Cup in September 2020?
Brighton 4-0 Portsmouth

3) Which team knocked Brighton out of the EFL Trophy at the Quarter Final stage in 2008?
Swansea City

4) Which Manchester City scored the only goal as Brighton lost in the 2019 FA Cup Semi Final?
Gabriel Jesus

5) Brighton had reached that stage by dramatically beating Millwall on penalties in the Quarter Final having drawn 2-2 in normal time thanks to late goals from which two players?
Jurgen Locadia and Solly March

6) Which lower-league club knocked Brighton out of the FA Cup at the First Round stage in November 2003?
Lincoln City

7) Who scored two own goals during the 6-1 FA Cup defeat to Liverpool in February 2012?
Liam Bridcutt

8) Which League Two team beat Brighton in the League Cup in August 2013?
Newport County

9) Which team did Brighton hammer 8-0 in the FA Cup in 2006?
Northwich Victoria

10) Which Premier League side did Brighton knock out of the FA Cup in both 2012 and 2013?

Newcastle United

Memorable Games Answers

1) Who scored the winner as Brighton won 2-1 at Crystal Palace in March 2019?
Anthony Knockaert

2) Which team did Brighton beat 5-0 at home in League One in March 2009?
Yeovil Town

3) Which Manchester City player was sent off before The Seagulls fought back from 2-0 down to win 3-2 in May 2021?
Joao Cancelo

4) Who scored the equaliser against Ipswich on the final day of the 2004/05 Championship season to ensure the club avoided the drop?
Adam Virgo

5) Who scored a hat-trick as Brighton beat Leyton Orient 5-0 on New Year's Day in 2011?
Glenn Murray

6) Brighton beat Fulham 5-0 in April 2016 thanks to a hat-trick from Tomer Hemed, and goals from Anthony Knockaert and which other player?
Bruno

7) By what score-line did Brighton beat Blackpool at home in the Championship in April 2013?
6-1

8) Which defender scored the only goal as Crystal Palace were beaten 1-0 at Selhurst Park in October 2005?
Paul McShane

9) Bobby Zamora scored three times in an entertaining 6-2 win over which team in September 2000?
Torquay United

10) Who scored twice during the 3-0 win over Spurs in October 2019?
Aaron Connolly

Red Cards Answers

1) Which two Brighton players were sent off during the 2-1 defeat at Wolves in May 2021?
Lewis Dunk and Neal Maupay

2) Who was given his marching orders following a tangle with Adebayo Akinfenwa in a 1-1 draw with Northampton in 2009?
Adam Virgo

3) Lewis Dunk was sent off late on in the 1-1 draw with Crystal Palace in October 2020 for a lunge on which player?
Gary Cahill

4) Gary Hart was dismissed for elbowing an opposition player in a 3-2 defeat to which team in February 2003?
Wimbledon

5) Brighton lost 3-0 to which side in February 2006 after Adam Hinshelwood was shown two yellow cards?
Norwich

6) Who was shown a straight red for a reckless challenge in the 2-0 home loss to Southampton in August 2019?
Florin Andone

7) Who scored but was then dismissed in the 1-1 Championship draw with Middlesbrough in 2016?
Dale Stephens

8) Andrew Crofts was sent off against which Championship club in August 2014?
Sheffield Wednesday

9) Brighton managed to beat Crystal Palace 3-1 in December 2018 despite which defender being shown a red card in the first half?
Shane Duffy

10) Ben White was sent off against which team in April 2021?

Chelsea

Managers Answers

1) Who was the Brighton manager at the start of the 21st century?
Micky Adams

2) What was the result in Steve Coppell's last game in charge before he left for Reading?
Brighton 3-0 Blackpool

3) Who took over as permanent manager from Coppell in 2003?
Mark McGhee

4) Who was in charge as Brighton avoided relegation from League One in 2009?
Russell Slade

5) Which team did Brighton beat 3-1 away from home in Gus Poyet's first game as manager?
Southampton

6) Gus Poyet was replaced as manager by who in 2013?
Oscar Garcia

7) Who was placed in caretaker charge after Sami Hyypia left the club?
Nathan Jones

8) Chris Hughton appointed who as his assistant manager in February 2015?
Colin Calderwood

9) Hughton guided the club to their first ever Premier League win with victory over which team in September 2017?
West Brom

10) Graham Potter started off his reign with a victory away at Watford by what score-line?
Watford 0-3 Brighton

First Goals Answers

1) Bobby Zamora
   Plymouth Argyle

2) Leon Knight
   Oldham Athletic

3) Colin Kazim-Richards
   Coventry City

4) Glenn Murray
   Crewe Alexandra

5) Lewis Dunk
   Cheltenham Town

6) Leonard Ulloa
   Arsenal

7) Ashley Barnes
   Tranmere Rovers

8) Anthony Knockaert
   Brentford

9) Neal Maupay
   Watford

10) Alireza Jahanbakhsh
    Bournemouth

Transfers 2011-2021 Answers

1) From which team did Brighton buy Will Buckley in June 2011?
Watford

2) Which Dutch forward signed from Excelsior in July 2011?
Roland Bergkamp

3) From which club did Will Hoskins arrive on a free in 2011?
Bristol Rovers

4) Club legend Bruno was signed back in 2012 from which Spanish side?
Valencia

5) Who was sold to Cardiff City in August 2012?
Craig Noone

6) Matthew Upson signed on a free transfer from which club in 2013?
Stoke City

7) Who was sold to Sunderland in the January transfer window of 2014?
Liam Bridcutt

8) Which goalkeeper arrived from Fulham in 2014?
David Stockdale

9) Which two players left to join Leicester City in July 2014?
Matthew Upson and Leonardo Ulloa

10) Brighton bought which Shrewsbury player in August 2015?
Connor Goldson

11) From which club was Pascal Gross bought in May 2017?
Ingolstadt

12) Goalkeeper Matt Ryan arrived from which team in 2017?
Valencia

13) Who arrived from Viktoria Plzen in the summer of 2017?

Ales Mateju

14) Which club did Kazenga Lua Lua leave for in January 2018?

Sunderland

15) From which club was Alireza Jahanbakhsh bought in July 2018?

AZ Alkmaar

16) Who was sold to Sheffield United in the winter transfer window of 2019?

Oliver Norwood

17) Brighton signed which player from PSG in August 2019?

Romaric Yapi

18) Aaron Mooy left to join which Chinese team in 2020?

Shanghai SIPG

19) Jose Izquierdo joined which team on a free after leaving Brighton in 2021?
Club Brugge

20) Which player signed from Ajax in July 2021?
Kjell Scherpen

If you enjoyed this book please consider leaving a five star review on Amazon

Books by Jack Pearson available on Amazon:

Cricket:

Cricket World Cup 2019 Quiz Book
The Ashes 2019 Cricket Quiz Book
The Ashes 2010-2019 Quiz Book
The Ashes 2005 Quiz Book
The Indian Premier League Quiz Book

Football:

The Quiz Book of Premier League Football Transfers
The Quiz Book of the England Football Team in the 21st Century
The Quiz Book of Arsenal Football Club in the 21st Century
The Quiz Book of Aston Villa Football Club in the 21st Century
The Quiz Book of Chelsea Football Club in the 21st Century
The Quiz Book of Everton Football Club in the 21st Century

The Quiz Book of Leeds United Football Club in the 21st Century

The Quiz Book of Leicester City Football Club in the 21st Century

The Quiz Book of Liverpool Football Club in the 21st Century

The Quiz Book of Manchester City Football Club in the 21st Century

The Quiz Book of Manchester United Football Club in the 21st Century

The Quiz Book of Newcastle United Football Club in the 21st Century

The Quiz Book of Southampton Football Club in the 21st Century

The Quiz Book of Sunderland Association Football Club in the 21st Century

The Quiz Book of Tottenham Hotspur Football Club in the 21st Century

The Quiz Book of West Ham United Football Club in the 21st Century

The Quiz Book of Wrexham Association Football Club in the 21st Century

Printed in Great Britain
by Amazon

50881710R00030